Great Personalities of India

Veer Shivaji

Simran

DIAMOND BOOKS

ISBN : 978-81-288-3621-3

Publisher : **Diamond Pocket Books (P) Ltd.**
X-30, Okhla Industrial Area, Phase-II
New Delhi-110020
Phone : 011-40712200
E-mail : wecare@diamondbooks.in
Website : www.diamondbooks.in
Edition : 2026
Printed by : Repro (India)

Veer Shivaji

By- *Simran*

Contents

Introduction

The name of Indian valiant Chhatrapati Shivaji will always be mentioned with huge regard and respect. The name is inscribed in gold in Indian history books. Shivaji was widely known for his bravery yet gentle behaviour. Establishing a sovereign Hindu state was almost an impossible dream for the Marathas. However, Chhatrapati Shivaji made this impossible dream into reality with his consistent struggle, strong will-power and bravery.

Chhatrapati Shivaji, the brave warrior and patriot fought with Mughals and founded the Hindu Maratha kingdom against all odds. This legendary warrior inspired and united the common man to rise against the tyranny of Aurangzeb, the Mughal ruler of that era. Shivaji Maharaj instilled a feeling of self-pride and nationality in common man.

Chhatrapati Shivaji raised a very strong army and navy out of nothing. He constructed

forts and new buildings that became major landmarks in Maratha and Indian history. The popular revenue collection system was introduced by Shivaji. Harassment in the name of revenue collection was strictly banned by this humble Maratha ruler. The teachings of mother Jijabai and mentor Dada Konddeo instilled moral values in Shivaji and inspired him to fight against the strong and widespread Mughal rulers.

The Birth of a Legendary Warrior

Many centuries ago, when India was under the tyranny of Mughal rule, a great warrior was born to create movement of freedom. This beautiful baby came to earth on 19th February, 1630 to Shahji Bhosle and Jijabai. It was a grand moment for Shivneri Fort.

The Dhai ma came to Jijabai with the baby and said, Look how lovely your baby is, Jijabai! He will make you proud one

day.ƒ This was a moment of mixed feelings for mother Jijabai. All was not well between Jijabai and her husband. Shahji was always on the battleground fighting for the Sultan. He did not care much about his wife. Jijabai wanted to share the news of birth of their son with Shahji.

Please send a message to the father of baby immediately!ƒ ordered Jijabai to the Dhai ma. Jijabai was a strong woman. She decided to make a great personality out of her son. People welcomed this baby with rolling of drums and celebrations.

Struggling Childhood of Maratha King

Shivaji did not have a happy childhood. His father was away from him. Mother Jijabai had come to live with Dada Konddeo, the caretaker of Shahji s Pune land. Jijabai s father Lukji Jadhavrao was a chieftain of Nizamshah. After many years

of service, he left the post to join Mughal emperor Shahjehan.

Nizamshah could not tolerate this insult. I will take my revenge,ƒ thought Nizamshah. He immediately called in for a meeting of all Jadhav chiefs at Daulatabad on 25th of July, 1629. The meeting was just a wicked plan by Nizamshah. When Jhadavrao arrived for the meeting with his sons, grandsons and all chiefs, Nizamshah s soldiers killed them mercilessly.

Jijabai was deeply hurt by the death of her father, brothers and nephew. She resolved to avenge their death by ending Mohammaden rule in the region. I swear to destroy Nizamshah s rule forever. My son will fight against them,ƒ she resolved.

Secret Dwelling of Young Veer Maratha

Shivaji s father Shahji was busy fighting against the Mughals for Nizamshah. The

Mughal emperor was successful in occupying the Fort of Daulatabad. He ordered his chief, Mahadal Khan to visit the Shivneri fort and capture Shahji s family.

Jijabai was a smart lady. She immediately sent Mahadal a message that she will come to meet him personally. Mahadal believed her. Meanwhile Jijabai prepared young Shivaji to be sent to a safe place with a maid. She said, I believe you. My son s life is in danger. You take him away and look after him.ƒ

The maid was faithful to her Madam. Don t worry, Maasaheb! I will take care of Shivaji as my own son,ƒ assured by maid. She took him away to an unknown place. For two long years, the maid took care of Shivaji. Shivaji called her Dhaima fondly. Jijabai who was captured by Mahadal escaped from his clutches after two years. Now she wanted to spend her time in looking after her son.

Dadaji Konddeo as a Mentor

After the end of Nizamshah rule, Shahji went to serve the Sultan of Bijapur in 1636. He got a huge piece of land as a gift by the Sultan in Pune. He immediately appointed faithful chiefs to take care of the the land. Dadaji Konddeo was the chief and most trusted caretaker of the land. Shahji sent Jijabai and Shivaji to Pune.

Dadaji Konddeo agreed to serve as a mentor to Shivaji. Shivaji was very happy to have such a great mentor in his life. Dadaji called him Shivba Raje with love. One day, Dadaji said to Shivaji, Shivba, I will teach you all that you need to become a strong warrior.ƒ Shivaji trusted his guide. In short time, Shivaji learnt to read and write. Dadaji Konddeo also taught him the art of fighting at the battlefield.

Shivaji was an intelligent student. He picked up all that was taught to him by Dadaji in a short span of time. Mother Jijabai

also contributed in the teachings of Shivaji. She narrated him tales from the Ramayana and Mahabharata. While narrating these tales, she instilled the qualities of bravery and fighting against injustice in young Shivaji.

Once, she told him, We are brave descendants of Lord Rama and brave Arjuna my son! We should not tolerate tyranny of strangers who rule us. We should fight for our freedom.ƒ

Young Shivaji could not understand the meaning of these words by Jijabai. He asked her mother, What freedom AaiSaheb? Whom should we fight with?ƒ Jijabai could not answer these innocent questions by his son.

Dadaji Konddeo happened to overhear the mother-son conversation. He saw this as an opportunity to enlighten Shivaji with the condition of their race and birth place. He said, Shivba Raje, You are very young now. You don t know what we are going through. Your father is a brave man. He is hiding himself to save his life. We are in exile. The Mughal emperor has taken everything from us. His personnel are causing devastation in our lands and forts. We are his slaves. They cheated your grandfather Jadhavrao and killed him, your uncle and cousins mercilessly. You must grow up strong and brave to fight this tyranny. Get freedom for your father, mother, me and your people.*f*

Shivaji was highly influenced by these words of his mentor. He resolved to fight against the Muslim rule all his life. Mother Jijabai and Dadaji Konddeo helped young Shivaji train under the best military commanders. He studied politics and religion.

Turning of Young Shivaji into Great Maratha Hero

Young Shivaji was deeply hurt by the story of devastation done by the Muslim rule in Pune and adjacent areas. He started devoting his time to form a new government for the well being of his people. Shivaji made efforts to remove lawlessness in his area. He made people aware of the tyranny they have been living under. People got highly influenced by Shivaji s patriotic feelings and joined him. This helped Shivaji to form a group that was ready to fight for freedom.

Shivaji was not satisfied with the small group against vast Muslim rule. He started roaming about at nearby areas. He asked people about their problems and fears. Shivaji assured them a better life via giving them their right to freedom. People were impressed by the efforts made by Shivaji for their well-being. They trusted him and wanted to join in the mission.

Dadaji Konddeo and mother Jijabai became his strength. Dadaji Konddeo took charge of one of the estates in Mawal and organized panchayats. Construction of new

ponds, and tanks went in progress to promote agriculture. Disputes were settled through panchayats.

Shivaji was formally dressed in royal robes by Dadaji Konddeo. He assured people about a happy and free life under the rule of Shivaji. This was the turning of young Shivaji into the hero of people around him.

The condition of state improved and people started leading a happier life. Shivaji and his decisions were respected by all.

The Rising of Maratha Power

Shivaji devoted most of his time in the establishment of an independent Hindu state. His childhood friends who were very close to him were ready to participate in the movement. They were ready to sacrifice their lives for Shivaji. One day, Shivaji and his friends went to a temple and pledged to fight for independent Hindu state.

We take oath that we will establish independent Hindu Swarajya,ƒ said Shivaji and dropped blood on the idol of lord Shiva. His friends joined in. We are with you Shivaji, always!ƒ replied his friends and dropped their share of blood on the idol.

This was the beginning of establishment of Maratha power. Shivaji formed a strong army of loyal and valiant soldiers. Shivaji decided to capture a few forts to start off the campaign.

The Torna Fort Capture

Shivaji attacked the Torna fort in 1646. The brave army of Shivaji help him to capture the fort easily. The sky roared with the voice Har Har mahadev! Shivaji Maharaj ki Jai!ƒ Shivaji was happy with this capture. He saw this as an opportunity to start a new kingdom referred to as Hindu Swaraj.

Shivaji wanted to threaten the Sultan of Bijapur, Muhammad Adil Shah by

capturing the fort. He thought of a plan to deceive the Sultan to capture more forts. He decided to send a message to the Sultan of Bijapur.

Message To Sultan of Bijapur

Shivaji had a clever plan in his mind to trick Sultan of Bijapur. He sent one of his messengers to the Sultan s court. Go! Give my message to the Sultan,ƒ said Shivaji to his messenger. As your wish, your Highness!ƒ replied the messenger.

At the Sultan s court, the messenger said, I have a message from Shivaji, my Lord!ƒ The Sultan was puzzled at this. What is it?ƒ he roared angrily. The messenger read the message sent from Shivaji, I have captured the Torna, Jahanpanah. I did it only for your good. You will certainly benefit from this.ƒ

The Sultan could not understand this puzzle. What benefit will I get from this capture? What Shivaji wants from me?ƒ

shouted Sultan at the messenger. The messenger said, My lord, let me read the message in full.ƒ He read the message further. The message said:

The people here are not dedicated to the Fort. It is empty without any security. They are also not ready to pay their dues to you. Capturing this Fort will help you get what is rightfully deserved to you. I am always at your service.ƒ This message made the Sultan happy. He did not suspect his character.

This was a turning point in Shivaji s career. He took this as an opportunity to build a strong army for himself. He reconstructed the Fort to secure it from enemies. The Sultan of Bijapur was again sent a message. Shivaji made Sultan believe that construction was being carried forward for security of the State.

Death of Dadaji Konddeo

After the capture of Torna fort, Dadaji Konddeo passed away on 7th March, 1647. This was a sad phase in Shivaji s life. Dadaji helped Shivaji to reach where he was today. Just when he was near his destination, Dadaji left for heavenly abode.

Dadaji called Shivaji before his death and said, Shivba Raje! The time has come. I have to take your leave. The responsibility is on your shoulders now. I directed you to your purpose. You have reached very near to your destination. The Hindu Swarajya has been built. You need to protect it and help it grow bigger and stronger.ƒ

I would do as you say Dadasaheb! I will fulfil your dream to create a powerful Hindu Samrajya for you, me and our people,ƒ said Shivaji as tears rolled down his cheeks. Shivaji was devastated by the death of Dadaji. He loved him more than his father. He was his father, mentor and friend.

Shivaji was influenced by the last words of Dadaji. He wanted to fight and win for Dadaji, mother Jijabai and his people suffering from the tyranny of Mughal rule.

Capturing Chakan

Shivaji looked forward to capture the Fort of Chakan. This was a necessary step for him to remove revolting officers and chiefs of Chakan from his path. Shivaji was a clever ruler. He was a great politician too. He knew when to use wits and when take up a sword.

Firangji Narsal, the guard of Chakan Fort was the main target of Shivaji to capture the Fort successfully. He influenced him by his words. Soon Narsal went into favour of Shivaji. This helped him to capture the fort without any difficulty. The fort finally came under Shivaji s rule in the year 1648. Pune went into the mood of celebration.

Shivaji appointed Narsal as the chieftain of the Chakan fort. He was assigned the duty of managing crucial task of revenue collection in villages and areas around the Fort. Shivaji s capture came as a challenge to Bijapur.

Furious Sultan of Bijapur

The activities of Shivaji created a revolutionary impact among his people and neighbouring states. The Sultan of Bijapur got news of Shivaji s exploits. He was furious. He immediately ordered his army to stop Shivaji s activities. The man is becoming a nuisance for us. It is time to put an end to his activities. Stop him now!!ƒ said the Sultan to his messenger. He sent a warning to Shivaji.

Shivaji was not alone. He had a powerful army now with huge support of his followers. He did not fear the Sultan anymore. Shivaji s aim was to capture Bijapur. I want to progress towards my biggest aim now! I will throw the Sultan away!ƒ said Shivaji to himself. He captured

many more forts including Supa, Purandar and Singhgarh.

The Sultan got news of Shivaji s determination to face the challenge. He panicked. Sultan had many dedicated followers. They could easily sacrifice their lives for Sultan. Afzal Khan, his shrewd general was one of them.

The Terror of Afzal Khan

Afzal Khan was known for his steadfast skills and efficient commanding ability. Sultan of Bijapur was happy with his services and offered him the highest rank among his officers. He was bestowed with the title of Mansabdar (commander) by the Sultan.

Afzal Khan was famous for his cruelty and fierce nature. He was also known as a slayer of Kafirs. The overall personality of Afzal Khan was dreaded by all. He was a giant of a man and about 7 feet tall. His

built was proportional to his height. He towered over everyone. It was said that Shivaji only reached him up to his chest. Hindu s feared Afzal s fierce nature and cruelty. He was also awarded a popular sword 'Adili'. This was a huge diamond studded sword. The famous elephant Howdah named Dhal-Gaj was also bestowed on Afzal as a gift for his brave deeds and services to Sultan. He was popular for destruction around him. He destroyed all Hindu temples on the way to Pratapgadh.

The Sultan of Bijapur was sure that Afzal Khan was the right person to defeat Shivaji. He ordered Afzal Khan to teach a lesson to Shivaji. You will see Shivaji dead soon, your Highness,ƒ assured Afzal to the Sultan. The Sultan was very happy with Afzal s confidence. He stayed assured of defeating Shivaji with Afzal on his side.

Afzal Khan's Plan to Trap Veer Shivaji

Shivaji had a small yet strong army. It helped him win many battles in the mountainous terrains of Sahyadri Mountain Range. Afzal Khan watched the actions of Shivaji for some time to understand his strategy. He wanted Shivaji to have an encounter with him in the open. Afzal Khan had a plan in his mind. He started doing things to provoke Shivaji to challenge him openly. He destroyed temples and forts.

However, Shivaji was a clever politician. He understood that Afzal Khan was sent to stop him and his activities. He decided to teach Afzal Khan a lesson. Shivaji immediately sent a message to Afzal Khan.

A messenger immediately visited Afzal Khan s court. I have a message from Shivaji Maharaj for you, my Lord,ƒ said the messenger to Afzal Khan. What is it?ƒ asked confused Afzal Khan.

The message read: Dear Afzal Khan, I m tired of the battles and destruction. I have a small army and cannot fight a huge warrior like you. I want to protect my people. Please meet me alone for a negotiation. I am not capable of fighting with such a huge army as yours. Shivaji.ƒ

Afzal Khan was happy to hear this message. He is afraid of my army. At last! I have conquered. Now it is my chance to please the Sultan by killing this mouse,ƒ said Afzal Khan to himself. Afzal asked the messenger to tell Shivaji that he has accepted the proposal.

Shivaji's Victory over Cruel Afzal Khan

Shivaji was happy to hear that Afzal Khan agreed to the proposal. The two decided to meet him in the foot hills of Fort Pratapgadh. Afzal Khan saw this as a great opportunity to kill Shivaji. He plotted the murder.

Shivaji was brave yet clever. His lessons in politics and teachings from Dadaji Konddeo made him a valiant and wise warrior. He could understand the intentions behind Afzal s excitement to meet him. He prepared himself well in advance for the meeting.

At last the fateful day of meeting came on November 30, 1659. Shivaji Maharaj prepared himself like a true warrior going for a battle. He wore a chilkhat (armor) under his clothes. He wore his favourite weapon, the wagh nakh (tiger claws) in his hands. It was covered with rings.

Shivaji entered the tent of Afzal Khan. Afzal pretended to be very happy to meet shivaji. I m delighted to meet a great warrior like you, said Afzal to Shivaji.

The tales of your valour have reached my ears. I am also happy to meet a great personality like you,ƒ replied Shivaji.

Let s start the saga of our friendship with embrace. Come! Let us get closer,ƒ said

Afzal Khan. Afzal Khan embraced Shivaji. Seeing the opportunity, Afzal immediately gripped Shivaji s neck under his left arm. He struck him with the dagger in his back.

The armor Shivaji wore saved him. In retaliation, Shivaji used his tiger claws and cut open Afzal Khan s stomach. Ya Allah! I m betrayed! I m betrayed,ƒ screamed Afzal Khan. He stumbled down.

Shivaji immediately ordered his body guards to spread the message of Afzal Khan s death. Afzal khan s head was cut off from his body and presented to mother Jijabai on a plate. This was a message from Shivaji to his mother that the end of Mughal army is about to come. Afzal s army panicked to know about his death. They surrendered to Shivaji.

Attack on Siddhi Johar

Shivaji continued his spree of attacks on the Mughals after attaining victory over cruel Afzal Khan. He recaptured the Forts of Vasantgarh, Raangana and many others that were earlier taken over by Afzal Khan. Thereafter, he progressed towards his mission of entering the Mughal territory.

He reached Panhala in Kolhapur district. He camped in the fort. This was seen as a great opportunity by Siddhi Johar, the chief officer of Karnul Province to trap Shivaji. He surrounded the fort with his huge army.

Now, Shivaji is trapped for sure! There is no escape for him,ƒ said Siddhi Johar to his soldiers. Siddhi Johar s siege at the fort lasted for more than four months. Shivaji acted with patience. He knew how to tackle the shrewd Siddhi Johar.

At last, monsoon arrived. Shivaji made a daring plan. I will send a message across to Siddhi Johar. He will be happy.ƒ He sent a message to Siddhi Johar that read Shivaji wanted to surrender.

Siddhi Johar was elated at this news. Ah! Our efforts and long waiting have given us fruit of success. He has given up, finally!ƒ said Siddhi Johar to himself.

The news of Shivaji s surrender spread like wild fire throughout the fort. The army relaxed after hearing the news. Shivaji Maharaj was happy to see this. He saw a wonderful opportunity one day. It was raining heavily that night and the army was in relaxing mode. Shivaji and his army of thousand soldiers escaped the fort.

The army headed to Vishalgarh with Bajiprabhu Deshpande. Baji Prabhu Deshpande was one of the brave lieutenants of Chattrapati Shivaji. Baji Prabhu helped Shivaji to escape from Panhala fort. He also kept constant watch on the army of Siddhi Johar. As soon as he sensed something wrong, he reported to Shivaji. Maharaj, we are being chased,ƒ he told Shivaji. Let us move ahead. I will defend you,ƒ assured Baji. Shivaji had full faith in his lieutenant. He did just as Baji directed him. Shivaji escaped the narrow pass near Vishalgarh with trusted men by his side. Meanwhile

Baji stayed on at the pass to fight those chasing Shivaji.

The army of Siddhi Johar soon reached the pass. There was a fierce battle between Siddhi Johar s army and Baji. Baji was a true warrior. He fought for Shivaji and his country bravely. He was determined to fight until Shivaji reaches Vishalgarh. His body was pierced by spears and arrows. But he continued fighting. I have to fight until Maharaj reaches Visahalgarh,ƒ Baji said to himself. After sometime, he heard the sound of cannon. He understood that Visahlgarh was welcoming Shivaji and his troop. He shouted, Har Har Mahadev! Jai Shivaji Maharaj!ƒ and breathed his last.

Baji was a true hero who sacrificed his life for the king and country. Shivaji got the news of Baji s sacrifice. He was deeply hurt. Shivaji named the Vishalgarh pass as Pawan Khindƒ as a tribute to Baji and his sacrifice.

Shivaji wanted to brings an end to the Mughal rule and death of brave warriors

under him. He concentrated on expanding his kingdom. His people were allowed equality. He also introduced friendly methods of revenue collection.

Shivaji and Shaista Khan

Aurangzeb, the Mughal ruler was keeping an eye on the activities of Shivaji. He knew that it was difficult to handle a clever ruler as Shivaji. The emperor wanted his nephew Shaista Khan to handle this matter. Call Shiasta Khan!ƒ the emperor ordered his men. As soon as Shaista Khan reached Aurangzeb, he ordered to destroy Shivaji. Go! Kill him and destroy his kingdom!ƒ said Aurangzeb.

Shaista Khan was a fierce officer to Aurangzeb. He was sent out to fight Shivaji with a huge army. In the year 1660, Shaista Khan arrived at Aurangabad. He swiftly captured Pune, Chakan, Kalyan and North Konkan Forts after a fierce battle with Shivaji s Maratha soldiers. Shaista Khan and his army banned the Marathas from entering Pune. Shivaji did not fear the terror and challenge of Shaista Khan. He was in the process of plotting against Shaista s army. Brave Shivaji created a strong army and prepared them for a surprise attack on Shaista s men.

On April 5, 1663, Shivaji and his army disguised themselves as participants at a wedding procession. Around 400 men participated in the procession and entered Pune. Shaista Khan and his army could not even imagine that something like this can arise in Shivaji s mind. At midnight, Shivaji and his army attacked and killed Mughal guards. Thereafter, they entered the palace of the Nawab and looked for Shaista Khan.

Shaista Khan was not prepared for this attack. He tried to run away from palace to save himself from the wrath of Shivaji. He tried to jump off a window in the palace. Shivaji attacked immediately. It was dark in the palace. Shivaji cut Shaista s thumb and two fingers of right hand with his sword. Shaista Khan fell unconscious. His son was killed during this attack.

Shivaji and his army escaped the palace in the dark. This sudden attack came as a great shock to Aurangzeb. He sent Shaista Khan back to Bengal. Shivaji recaptured all the forts seized by Shaista Khan. Aurangzeb knew that it was not the right time to challenge Shivaji s valour. He decided to wait and watch.

The Surat Loot

Shivaji s attack on forts and adjacent areas of Pune made him lose huge amount of wealth in building and maintaining a huge army. He found out a way to regain the lost wealth. Let us march towards Surat. The place is rich in wealth,ƒ ordered Shivaji to his generals. However, Shivaji s advisors were against the plan. Your Highness! We are with you. But you may make Aurangzeb more angry with this loot,ƒ told Shivaji s advisors to him.

Shivaji was in no mood to listen to his advisors. He wanted money to regain his strength and fight against the Mughal army. He marched towards Surat. The attack was successful. Shivaji looted Surat for about four days. He managed to collect huge wealth from this place.

Shivaji was a brave warrior yet a gentleman at heart. He ordered his generals not to harm women, children and the old during the loot.

Jai Singh's Revenge

Aurangzeb was very furious to know about Surat loot. He wanted to put an end to Shivaji s actions. He immediately called upon Raja Jai Singh to stop Shivaji. Jai Singh! Do whatever it takes to stop Shivaji and his army from further loots and attacks,ƒ said Aurangzeb to Jai Singh. Raja Jai Singh was determined to help Aurangzeb. He prepared a huge army and started capturing Shivaji s territory.

Shivaji took this as a great challenge and decided to stop Jai Singh. I must do something before it gets too late!ƒ said Shivaji to his courtiers. He sent his messenger with a special message to Raja Jai Singh. The message was about making peace among Shivaji Maharaj and Raja Jai Singh.

Soon a meeting was held and a treaty was agreed upon. Raja Jai Singh had other plans in his mind. He immediately invited Shivaji to meet the Emperor. Shivaji could not deny the proposal. He promised Raja Jai Singh to visit the Emperor.

Raja Jai Singh said, I will accompany with my son Ram Singh and want you to come along with your son, Sambhaji too. This will be a memorable meeting,ƒ said Raja Jai Singh to Shivaji Maharaj. Shivaji agreed to this.

When Shivaji s advisors heard about this, they became suspicious of Jai Singh s intentions. They warned Shivaji against Jai Singh, Your Highness! You should refrain yourself from visiting the emperor. This looks like a trap.ƒ

Shivaji could not do anything as he had already promised Jai Singh. As a true Maratha, he decided to keep honour of his words.

Lion in the Cage

Shivaji Maharaj reached Agra. He visited the Emperor to offer wishes on his birthday. Aurangzeb did not welcome Shivaji. He made Shivaji and his son stand among his lower grade commanders. Aurangzeb did not speak a word to Shivaji and kept himself busy in accepting gifts from generals and other visitors to the court.

Shivaji could not bear the insult anymore. I will not tolerate this insult. Come, my son! We will leave this place,ƒ said Shivaji to his son. However, Aurangzeb had already planned a trap for Shivaji. He was arrested and trapped inside Aurangzeb s palace.

Shivaji s son got scared. Oh father! We have been trapped. What can we do now?*f* he asked his father. Shivaji was a brave man and had strong heart. He assured his son, Don t worry my dear son! We will escape soon.*f*

Marvellous Escape of Shivaji

Aurangzeb hated Shivaji for his efforts towards putting an end to the Mughal rule and his popularity among common men. He decided to kill Shivaji and his son. Raja Jai Singh came to know of Aurangzeb s plans. He immediately sent a message to the emperor. He asked emperor to convince Shivaji to join his army and use his valour, strength and political skills to capture forts and lands in the southern area. He reminded Aurangzeb of Shivaji s political skills in killing of cruel Afzal Khan and defeat of Shaista Khan and Siddhi Johar.

Aurangzeb was influenced by Jai Singh s plans. He dropped his idea to assassinate

Shivaji and his son. He started making efforts towards convincing Shivaji to join his army by hook or by crook. Shivaji took this as an opportunity to escape. He made a plan. He started acting as if he had lost all hopes. Then suddenly he pretended to have fallen ill.

He requested Aurangzeb to be allowed to donate fruits and sweets to Brahmins so that they can pray for his speedy recovery. Aurangzeb wanted to please Shivaji and make him a part of his army. He agreed upon Shivaji s request. This became a daily routine. Huge baskets of fruits and sweets were sent out of the palace. During the first few days, these baskets were checked thoroughly. However, as days passed by the inspectors took it as a casual event and became careless.

One day, Shivaji hide himself and his son in two baskets. He made sure that good quantity of fruits and leaves were scattered around in the basket so that they could not be easily caught. Shivaji and his son

escaped the palace. The basket bearers left the baskets at a beautiful place in Agra and went away.

Shivaji and his son Sambhaji came out of the baskets in the dark and managed to get out of Agra safely. He went to Mathura to avoid people identify him. His son was a young boy of nine and could not join the struggle. He used to get tired easily. Shivaji decided to leave him with maternal uncle.

Thereafter, Shivaji shaved his head and beard off. He moved around in disguise of a saint from one place to another. He created army with trusted people. Shivaji s main concern was wealth. He gathered many disciples as a saint and accepted donations. Enough wealth was collected by Shivaji in a short period of time. Shivaji s trusted leaders and generals continued to rob villages to collect money for Shivaji.

On September 12th, 1666, Shivaji reached Maharashtra. He visited his mother Jijabai. Jijabai was a religious woman and

respected saints. As she was about to touch his feet, Shivaji bent down on his knees and said, Maasaheb, I m back.ƒ

Mata Jijabai was extremely happy to see her son after a long time. Tears of joy rolled down her cheeks as she embraced him. This was one of the happiest and touching moments in Jijabai s life.

Shivaji's Corronation

Shivaji soon started recapturing his forts. He decided to attack the Fort of Kondhana. Tanaji Malusare, the most trusted and efficient general of Shivaji was assigned this task. Tanaji was determined to make Shivaji proud. He set off for the battle with his army.

Tanaji decided to attack the Mughal army in the darkness of night. He ordered his forces to climb a huge wall of the fort. The battle soon started. The Mughal army was powerful and the battle got fierce. Valiant Tanaji and his brave officers managed to capture the fort. However, Tanaji lost his life during his battle. Shivaji was bereaved to hear the news of Tanaji s death.

Mother Jijabai wanted to see his son ruling an independent nation before she dies. She called upon a priest and asked Shivaji to get prepared for the coronation. She wanted to arrange for the coronation in a grand and royal way. Shivaji said, As you wish, Maasaheb! I will do as you desire.ƒ

The priest and Shivaji s courtiers arranged for a grand coronation. The event took place among thousands of Brahmins and more than fifty thousand spectators. A huge diamond studded throne was prepared for Shivaji. The palace was filled with sounds of spectators shouting Shivaji Maharaj ki Jai!*f*

Shivaji's Reign

Shivaji wanted to create a safe and strong kingdom for his people. He started ruling wisely. Muslims in his area were not slaughtered. Right to equality and freedom was respected. He allowed right to religion. None of the Mosques were destroyed. His main focus was to build a strong army against the Mughal rule. He refrained from attacking the Mughal territory for some years. Aurangzeb thought that Shivaji is no

more interested in the devastation of Mughal rule.

As his army became large and strong, he started recapturing his forts. He captured Khandesh, Berra, Vellore, Sondha, Karwar, Vendoor, Valingadapuram, Satara fort and Jinji. With the help of his huge and dedicated army, Shivaji managed to capture a major part of Mughal territory. People were very happy in Shivaji s reign.

Shivaji's Illness and Death

As Shivaji grew old, his health started deteriorating. He was upset about the death of his first wife Saibai. His son Sambhaji was not a man of character. He was not worthy of being his heir. His second wife

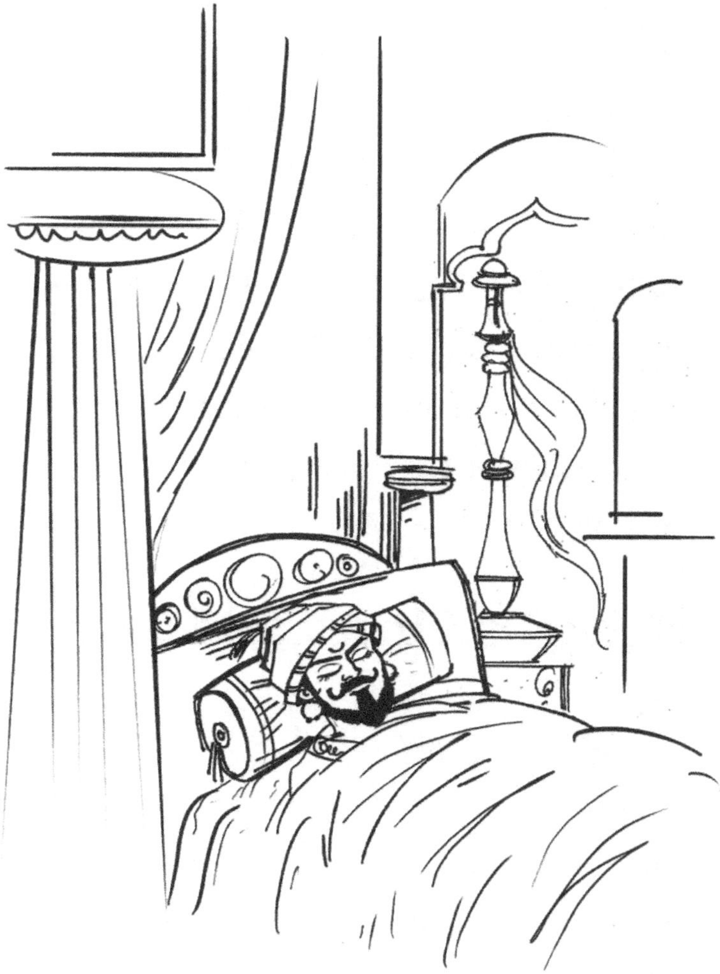

Soyarbai constantly fought with him to make her son Rajaram, the heir prince.

One day, Shivaji suffered from high fever and dysentery. He could not recover from fever which continued for many days. At last on 3rd April 1680, Shivaji breathed his last. The great conqueror slept forever. The whole kingdom mourned.

❑❑❑